○ Collin

D0539578

The Voices of Children

by
Michael Morpurgo

Resource Material by
Michael Goron

William Collins' dream of knowledge for all began with the publication of his first book in 1819. A self-educated mill worker, he not only enriched millions of lives, but also founded a flourishing publishing house. Today, staying true to this spirit, Collins books are packed with inspiration, innovation and a practical expertise. They place you at the centre of a world of possibility and give you exactly what you need to explore it.

Collins. Do more.

Published by Collins
An imprint of HarperCollinsPublishers
77–85 Fulham Palace Road
Hammersmith
London
W6 8JB

Browse the complete Collins catalogue
at www.collinseducation.com

Playscript copyright © Michael Morpurgo 2007.

10 9 8 7 6 5 4 3 2 1

ISBN-13   978 000 7263462
ISBN-10   0-00-7263465

British Library Cataloguing in Publication Data

A Catalogue record for this publication is available from the British Library

Commissioned by Charlie Evans
Design by JPD
Cover design by Paul Manning
Production by Simon Moore
Printed and bound by Martins the Printers

Acknowledgements

Photo credits: Mary Evans Picture Library p: 36, 40, 47, 49, 52, 54, 58, 59, 61. PA Photos p66.

Text credits: © p10: 'I am ful yong', The Dance of Death, Florence Warren (ed) 1931; p11: 'Young babes are and little children are simple...' is abridged from Two Sermons Preached by the Boy Bishop, Camden Society, new series 14 (1875); p12: 'Each time and season...bladder for to smite' is abridged from The Ecologues of Alexander Barclay (ed Beatrice White, London 1928); p18: 'Holy Thursday' by William Blake is from *Songs of Experience*; 'The Echoing Green' by William Blake is from *A Selection of Poems and Letters*, P27; 'The Children of the Windrush' is by Valerie Bloom, copyright HarperCollins, 2008; pp44–45: extract from *The Penguin Book of Childhood*, ed. Michael Rosen, 1995, © Penguin Books; p53: Henry Mayhew, London Labour and the London Poor, Volume 3, 1851; 'The Chimney Sweeper' by William Blake is from *A Selection of Poems and Letters*; p63–4: extract is taken from *The Invention of Childhood*, edited by Hugh Cunningham, © BBC Books, 2006; p66 extract from *Windrush: The Irrisistible Rise of Multi-racial Britain* by M. Philips and T. Philips, copyright HarperCollins, 1999; 'My Memories' is reproduced from *The Penguin Book of Childhood*, ed. Michael Rosen, 1995 © Penguin Books

Whilst every effort has been made both to contact the copyright holders and to give exact credit lines, this has not proved possible in every case.

Contents

PLAYSCRIPT

RESOURCES

Author's introduction

In helping to create for radio 'The Invention of Childhood', a series based largely on the research in this book, I have discovered a whole world I previously knew very little about. I had been a child, a father, a teacher, and a grandfather. I've lived and worked amongst children all my life. I also write about them a great deal, because I thought I knew them and had some insight into their world. I know them a lot better now.

Any book is a voyage of discovery, for the reader, but more particularly for the writer. For me 'The Invention of Childhood' has been like a journey to the centre of the child. What I learned on my journey was that childhood itself has changed over the centuries, and thankfully very much for the better, but that children haven't. How do I know this? From the children themselves, from children's voices speaking to us down the centuries. It is children who have informed and inspired this story, this history. So I thought it only right and proper to let the children speak for themselves, to let them have the first word.

Characters

HUGH

BEATY

CEDD

HEDDA

JOHN

ALEXANDER

ABIGAIL

GEOFFREY

MICHAEL

NEHEMIAH'S FATHER

NEHEMIAH

WILLIAM

JOAN

PIERS

ELIZABETH

GEORGE

SARAH

JIM

DR BANARDO

JAMES

VALERIE

CHARIS

The Voices of Children

Time: now.

Place: the communal gardens in an appartment block in West London.

Centre stage is a great uprooted oak tree, the massive root system facing the audience.

Beneath the roots is a large crater.

A children's birthday party is in full swing (the children aged between 10 and 12). There's a game of musical chairs going on without the chairs. 25 children are there, in historical costumes of various periods from Anglo-Saxon to medieval to Victorian, except for two, **Hugh** *aged 11 dressed as Bart Simpson and his sister* **Beaty** *dressed as Marge Simpson. Both are wearing easily identifiable cut out cardboard hairpieces. They are dancing, with the others, around in a circle (***Hugh*** obviously unwilling) to the strains of Boney M. The mood is wild. The music stops. Last to sit down is* **Hugh** *because he isn't paying attention. Cries of 'Hugh! Hugh!' He is out. He stomps off, fed up. The dancing circle continues with the music and then unravels, leaving* **Hugh** *alone with the tree. He sits down on the edge of the crater, disconsolate, chucking stones at the roots. We hear the music stop again.* **Beaty** *joins him, really fed up.*

Hugh	I wasn't trying anyway.
Beaty	Nor me.
Hugh	*(still chucking stones)* I could kill her.

BEATY	Who?
HUGH	Mum. I told her didn't I? Historical. The costumes for the party had to be historical. But she always knows best, doesn't she?
BEATY	Tell me about it.
HUGH	*(mimicking his mother, sarcastically)* 'Oh no, Hugh. I talked to Jamie's grandma about it, and she definitely said hysterical not historical. And hysterical, dear, means funny, if you didn't know. And Bart Simpson's funny – you're always telling me.' And then she goes and makes me wear this...thing. *(he whips off his head piece and hurls it into the crater, and **Beaty** does the same in solidarity)* I'll kill her.
BEATY	You're not allowed.
HUGH	And that's another thing. Why should she tell me what to wear anyway? They're always making the rules. Dad's just as bad. It's all they do, sit around making rules and drinking cups of coffee.
BEATY	We've got to have rules. It's like the days of the week. Monday and Tuesday and that. You wouldn't know when to go to school 'else. They are sort of like birthdays. You can't grow older unless you have birthdays, can you?
HUGH	Who wants to be old anyway? You get all wrinkly and you get hairs in your ears like grandpa. No thank you! You know what I want? I want to stay twelve years old

forever, and make up my own rules. And the first rule will be that I make the rules.

BEATY   *(not listening, she is looking at the fallen oak tree)* It's sad.

HUGH   What is?

BEATY   That tree. It got old, didn't it. I really loved it. It was the oldest in London Mum said. Been here forever.

HUGH   Couldn't have been for ever. Nothing's for ever is it? *(he's gazing at the upturned roots)* There's hundreds and hundreds of roots. Which was the first, I wonder?

BEATY   And who planted it?

*Enter silently, and without them noticing them, a sturdy looking eleven-year-old Anglo-Saxon boy, **Cedd**. He is scantily clad in furs. **Cedd** will serve as the narrator/chorus throughout the play, donning different period costumes on stage, as the centuries pass.*

CEDD   I did. I planted it. *(he bends down and picks up an acorn)* With this. Then when I died, they buried me beside it because it was my tree. *(he scoops up a handful of earth, and lets it pour through his fingers)* Not a lot of me left, is there?

*Both children are terrified at the implication of what has just been said. They have backed away, **Hugh** hiding behind **Beaty** for protection.*

HUGH   *(whispering)* Who's he?

BEATY	He wasn't at the party?
HUGH	Is he a ghost or what?
BEATY	Think so, and he hasn't got many clothes on either. Looks like Stig of the Dump.
CEDD	You should plant another one.
BEATY	Why us?
CEDD	Because it was my tree and you are my descendants, my relations. You came from me, just like this tree came from an acorn. *(to Beaty)* You could plant it together, *(to Hugh)* and you could put the acorn in, dig the hole for it too. I always had to do the digging when I was your age. They always give us boys the dirty jobs, don't they?
HUGH	*(less fearful now, glad of the proffered solidarity)* Huh, tell me about it.
CEDD	All right, I will. You'd better sit down though, because it's quite a story.

Beaty and *Hugh* are nonplussed by this response, but they sit on the edge of the crater. Just as they do so, onto the stage come all the 'party' children, ghosts now everyone of them, and moving slowly. *Beaty* and *Hugh* are alarmed. They can see the transition and know what it means.

CEDD	It's my story, and your story and their story too. They were there. They'll tell you all about it. They'll tell it as they found it, as they saw it, as it happened. And they are all your descendants, like me. But it's the story

of all the children who have known this land and breathed this air. It begins with me. I was digging a grave. My own little sister's grave. She was called Hedda.

*From the chorus comes a diminutive Anglo-Saxon girl, **Hedda**, very frail and pale. As with all the children from the chorus who come forward, she speaks directly to the audience, as do all the other ghost children when their turn comes.*

HEDDA   I am ful yong.
I was born yesterday.
Deth is ful hasty.
On me to ben werke.

*As **Hedda** rejoins the chorus, the chorus of children sing:*

CHORUS   Matthew, Mark, Luke and John,
Bless the bed that I lie on.
Four corners to my bed,
Four angels round my head.
One to watch, and one to pray,
And two to bear my soul away.

This verse is repeated.

CEDD   *(wearing a medieval costume now)* More than anything it was hunger and cold that took us young, took us from our families, took us from this world. Every mother, every father, every sister, every brother, knew the pity of it. It went on like this for hundreds of years, a massacre of the innocents. We had a day of our very own, a day to remember how King Herod had killed all the innocent children, but it was a day when we remembered all the children. Childermas it was called, December 28th every year, one day when we could be just who we wanted to be. It was a day when we could say what we liked, a day a boy could be a bishop, and even give a sermon, like John did in Gloucester Cathedral in front of hundreds of people. He told them.

John, escorted by two other children comes forward from the chorus. He's in tattered clothes. They dress him up like a bishop, and give him a bishop's mitre and crook. The mitre is too big and slips down over his face. They try again to put it on but it won't stay up. So his escorts hold it up for him as he gives his sermon. He does this with bishoplike pomposity, but he means every word.

JOHN 'Young babes and little children are simple, without gyle, innocent, without harme and all pure without corruption. You should perceive in them no manner of malice, nor envy, no disdayne, no hurtfulness, no synfull affection, no pride, no ambition, no singularities, no desire of honour, of riches, of carnality, of revenging, of quitting evil for evil.'

Chorus sings 'The Coventry Carol'

CEDD The trouble was, once the day was over, we were treated just the same as we had been before, worked to the bone, beaten whenever they felt like it. But once out of sight we could be children again. We could wander where we wanted, do what we pleased, play blind man's buff and hide and seek – and football too.

HUGH   Football!?

CEDD   They made it out of a pig's bladder. Alexander and Peter will tell you how it was.

Alexander and Peter, quite well-to-do medieval children, step forward to declaim this poem, a couplet each miming, quite comically the other's couplet.

ALEXANDER   Eache time and season hath its delites and
                    joys,
                Loke in the streets beholde the little boys.

                How in fruit season for joy they sing and
                    hop
                Lent is eache one full busy with his top.

                And now in winter for all the grievous colde
                Al rent and ragged a man may them
                    beholde.

                They have great pleasour, supposing well
                    to dine
                When men be busied in killing of fat swine.

                With many beans and peasen put within
                It rattleth, soundeth and shineth cleere and
                    fayre.

                When it is throwen and caste up in the ayre
                Each one contendeth and hath a great delite
                With foote and with hande the bladder for to
                    smite.

CEDD	Girls didn't play football. They didn't have nearly so much fun as boys did.
BEATY	Tell me about it!
CEDD	*(still not understanding this phrase)* Abigail knows all about it, don't you, Abigail? She was made to learn this and recite often, so she'd be a good girl, weren't you Abigail?
ABIGAIL	*(coming forward demurely and speaking very properly)* In temperate and patient innocence With modesty of bearing and of dress And showed in speech a modesty no less She used no fancy term in affectation Of learning, but according to her station She spoke, in all and everything she said She showed she was good and gently bred.
CEDD	And did you show you were good and gently bred?
ABIGAIL	*(screaming with frustration and rage and stamping her foot)* No! No! No!

She runs off the stage.

BEATY	Good for you.
CEDD	But there were rules for boys and girls alike.

Geoffrey and *Catherine* come forward.

GEOFFREY **CATHERINE**	*(in rather school marm voices)* Child, climb not over house nor wall, For no fruit, birds or ball. Child, over men's houses no stones fling Nor at glass windows no stones sling. And child, when thou goest to play Look thou come home by light of day.
CEDD	Then as if there weren't enough rules already, someone went and invented school. No one wanted to go. I mean, why did they do that?
HUGH	Dunno. I think they are still trying to work that out.

Michael comes forward looking doleful, rubbing his backside.

MICHAEL	My master looketh as he were mad 'Where hast thou been, thou sorry lad?' "Milking ducks", as my mother bade It was no marvel that I were sad. My master peppered my tail with good speed He would not leave till it did bleed Much sorrow hath he for his deed I would my mother were a hare And all his bookes greyhounds were And I myself a jolly hunter To blow my horn I would not spare For if he were dead I would not care!
BEATY	*(aside to **Hugh**)* They speak funny don't they?
HUGH	That's 'cos they always spoke in poetry in those days. He's getting changed again.

	Looks like a Tudor now. I done the Tudors in school – the Armada and that.
CEDD	*(changed again into Elizabethan costume)* I've always liked stories, bible stories, saints' stories, Robin Hood – if anyone should've been a saint, it was him, helping the poor like he did. But riddles were my favourite. Here, can you work this one out? Ready?
BEATY **HUGH**	*(together)* Ready.
CEDD	Two legs sat upon three legs With one leg in his lap. In comes four legs And runs away with one leg Up jumps two legs Catches up three legs Throws it after four legs And makes him bring back one leg.

*(**Beaty** and **Hugh** are stumped)*

You do go to school, do you? *(they nod)*
Well they didn't teach you much then, do
they? Watch this.

*The riddle is now acted out by the children for their benefit. **Simon** comes on with a three legged stool, sits on it. He has a leg of mutton in his lap. Dog comes in (**Abigail** on 4 legs) snatches leg of mutton and runs off stage. **Simon** throws stool off stage at dog who comes back on, tail between legs and brings back bone, licked clean. Dog tries to look happy and contrite at the same time.*

CEDD   See? Good, eh?

BEATY	Were they really all our relations?
CEDD	Every one of them, including the dog. *(suddenly serious)* They couldn't all play silly games though. Lots of our relatives never lived to grow up. Nehamiah she died when she was very little. These were the last words she ever spoke…

Nehamiah comes on – in nightclothes, supported by her father.

NEHEMIAH	Father I go abroad tomorrow and bring you a plum pie.
FATHER	*(as **Nehamiah** leaves him reluctantly, she lets go his hand)* Such a child I never saw, for such a child I bless God. Thou gavest her to us, thou hast taken her from us, blessed be the name of the Lord.

Cedd is shrugging on another costume, a boy of the civil war with a sword at his side.

CEDD	What do you think? *(he gives a twirl)*
BEATY	Cool.
HUGH	When are we now?
CEDD	Just after the Civil War, after they'd chopped off Charles I's head. The Royalists wore better clothes, but the Puritans won and unfortunately they were very keen on schools. So even more of us had to go to school now. *(**William** comes on, a boy, a Puritan)* But William was a farm boy, so he got lucky sometimes.

| **WILLIAM** | From the age of ten or twelve years we were very much better off the schoole. Espetialy in the Spring and Summer season, plou time, turfe time, hay time and harvest, looking after the sheep, helping at plough, making hay and shearing, two of us at thirteen or fourteen years-of-age being equal to one man shearer, so we made small progress in London, for what we get in winter we forget in summer. We got what writing we had in winter. *(sees schoolmaster coming)* Look out. Cave. Here's the master. I'm off. |

Alexander, dressed as school master, hurrying on, shaking his cane in fury after William. Seeing the audience suddenly, he remembers the dignity of his position. Mimicking a teacher.

| **ALEXANDER** | Obedience is one of the capital benefits arising from a public education, to break the ferocity of human nature, to subdue the passions, and to impress the principles of religion and morality – this is the first object to be attended by all schoolmasters who know their duty. William! *(he goes off stage)* William! Come back this minute, you rascal you! |
| **CEDD** | *(in 18th century coat and hat now)* But to be honest those children who were in school were the lucky ones – despite schoolmasters like him. You won't want to see this but you have to. It's part of the story. |

A poor mother comes on, carrying a baby in her arms. She looks around and then puts the baby down, kisses it, then runs off, weeping.

Many children were very poor, and poor meant hungry. Another mouth to feed was a mouth too many. Some were left in church porches. Worse still, some became beggars and a few even ended up as slaves. Slaves! Can you believe it?

*Two street children come on, **William** and **Joan**, one crouches to pick up the baby.*

HUGH	Who are they?
CEDD	Children who never lived to laugh and play. Listen.
WILLIAM	Is this a holy thing to see In a rich and fruitful land, Babes reduced to misery, Fed with cold and usurous hand?
JOAN	Is that trembling cry a song? Can it be a song of joy? And so many children poor? It is a land of poverty.
WILLIAM **JOAN**	And their sun does never shine, And their fields are black and bare, And their ways are filled with thorns; It is eternal winter there.
BEATY	They make me feel so sad. Are they our relations too?
CEDD	We all are.
HUGH	Were we always poor?

CEDD   No, but even if you weren't poor, children could have a hard time of it. Rules again. Rules, rules. Elizabeth was your great great grandmother – doesn't look like it, does she?

Elizabeth comes forward, middle class in her early teens, confident.

ELIZABETH   The milk rebellion was crushed immediately. In his dressing gown with his whip in his hand, father attended our breakfast… That disgusting milk! He began with me; my beseeching look was answered by a sharp cut, followed by as many more as were necessary to empty the basin. And bathtime was worse still. A large tub stood in the kitchen court, the ice on top of which had often to be broken before our horrid plunge into it. We were brought down from the very top of the house, four pairs of stairs, with only a cotton cloak over our nightgowns, just to chill us completely before the dreadful shock. How I screamed, begged, prayed, entreated to be saved, half the tender hearted maids in tears besides me, all to no use. Millar, our nurse had her orders.

CEDD   But once she got outside away from her father, away from the rules…

There follows a game of 'drop handkerchief'. Children (including Elizabeth), alternating girl/boy in a ring circling round. Elizabeth drops the handkerchief behind Piers's back. She runs off. Piers picks it up, is held by the girls on either side, so

Elizabeth can get away. He breaks free finally. She rejoins the ring just as he catches her. They go to the centre of the ring and kiss.

CEDD   That's Piers. And if you want to know, he became a relation as well, a little bit later.

The children, in nine couples, now come forward and recite a couplet each, before the next couple takes their place.

CHILDREN   The Sun does arise,
              And make happy the skies;

              The merry bells ring,
              To welcome the Spring;

              The sky-lark and thrush,
              The birds of the bush,

              Sing louder around
              To the bell's cheerful sound,

              Whilst our sports shall be seen
              On the Echoing Green.

              Old John with white hair,
              Does laugh away care,

              Sitting under the oak,
              Among the old folk.

              They laugh at our play,
              And soon they all say:

              'Such, were the joys,
              When we all, girls and boys,

Then all together.

In our youth time were seen,
On the Echoing Green.'

BEATY   Were they Victorians? We've done
Victorians in class, Oliver Twist and all that
stuff.

CEDD   *(donning a Victorian hat and coat)* We're
coming to them now. And you won't like
what you are going to hear. There never
was a worse time than this for children.
Children should be seen and not heard.
That's how they were treated up at the big
houses. And that was bad enough. *(**George**
comes on carrying his sweep's brushes over each
shoulder, blackened, coughing, exhausted)* For
the poor children, the working children, it
was a lot worse. This is George, he died
when he was eleven.

GEORGE   I was a climbing boy, I was. I was
apprentice to a master sweep. In Cambridge
it was. The last chimney I did was at
Fulbourne Hospital. I didn't want to go up
again. I was bad in my chest, see. But they
made me. They pricked the soles of my feet
to make me go up. They set straw alight
under me. I had to go up, didn't I? When I
died they opened me up and they found all
my lungs and my windpipe was full of
black powder. I suffocated to death,
couldn't breathe. It was good to die. Didn't
suffer no more after that.

CEDD   There were thousands of climbing boys like
George. Wherever they wanted cheap
labour they used children – in the factories
and the mills, down the mines, in the dirt

and the dark like Sarah – oh yes, girls too
went down the mines.

*Six children come in pushing a coal cart, all bent to their work, all
blackened, all barely able to keep going. They stop and lean on the
cart. One of them straightens herself slowly.*

SARAH   I work in the Gauper pit. I have to work
without a light and I'm scared. Sometimes I
sing when I've a light, but not in the dark. I
dare not sing then. I don't like being in the
pit. I'm very sleepy when I go sometimes in
the morning. I go to Sunday School and
read Reading Made Easy. I would like to be
at school far better than in the pit.

CEDD   Do you know the saddest story I ever
heard? It was about a factory girl who had
to get up early every morning to go to
work. One morning she was sick, too weak
to get up. She was lying in her father's
arms. She woke up and the first thing she
thought was that it must be time to go to
work. 'Father is it time?' she said. 'Father, is
it time?' Then she sank back in his arms
and died.

*Hear the sound of a drum and marching feet. A protest march of
ragged factory children, carrying banners reading 'Father is it
time?', 'Behold and Weep!' They all shout: 'No more! No more!
No more!' Then suddenly are still and silent. A single child,* **Clare,**
steps forward.

CLARE   The young lambs are bleating in the
meadows

The young birds are chirping in the nest
The young fawns are playing with the
    shadows,
The young flowers are blowing towards the
    West
But the young, young children, O my
    brothers,
They are weeping bitterly!
They are weeping in the playtime of the
    others
In the country of the free.

*Chorus of **children** pick up the echo of the last word and chant it, punching the air as they go off in time with the drumbeat of the protest march. 'Free! Free! Free! Free! Free!' **Hugh** and **Beaty** deeply upset and angry jump up and join in the chanting as the **children** leave.*

CEDD   There's more, *(**Hugh** and **Beaty** sit down again)* there were the street children like Jim. It was a cold winter's night and it was late. Look.

*Enter **Jim**, in rags, from stage left. He sits down hugging his knees, shivering. **Dr Barnardo**, (a child dressed up) comes from stage right. He notices **Jim** and goes over to him.*

DR BARNARDO Come my lad, had you not better get home. It's very late. Mother will be coming for you.

JIM   Please Sir, let me stop.

DR BARNARDO Why do you want to stay?

JIM   Please Sir, do let me stay. I won't do no harm.

Dr Barnardo   Your mother will wonder what kept you so late.

Jim   I ain't got no mother.

Dr Barnardo   Haven't got a mother, boy? Where do you live?

Jim   Don't live nowhere.

Dr Barnardo   Do you mean to say my boy that you have no home, that you have no mother or father?

Jim   That's the truth on't Sir. I ain't telling you no lie about it.

Dr Barnardo   But where did you sleep last night?

Jim   Down Whitechapel, Sir, in one of them carts as is filled with 'ay. I won't do 'arm Sir, if you let me stay.

Dr Barnardo   Are there other children sleeping out like you?

Jim   Oh yes lots, 'eaps on 'em, Sir. More'n I could count.

Dr Barnardo   You come along with me, lad. I'll find you somewhere warm, somewhere you can stay, and a good hot meal too.

Jim   Honest?

Dr Barnardo   Honest. *(he helps him up and they leave)*

Cedd   That was Dr Barnardo. He looked after thousands of street children just like Jim.

BEATY	So there were some good people?
CEDD	Lots of them, luckily for you. If there hadn't been, like as not you'd be living on the streets or working in factories still. Things got better all right. But not in a hurry. Look at your great grandfather now, James he was called. He was thirteen, first day at work.

James comes on, sees the audience, and stops to tell them. He's very pleased with himself – dressed in his new working clothes.

JAMES	Said goodbye to my schooling at Spotland Board School. Off to work at Heaps – fifty-five and a half hour working week for ten shillings and sixpence, a fortune for Mother. Mother rigged me out in this at a total cost of 15 shillings. Not bad, eh? *(does a turn)* Corduroy trousers, leather braces. Brown cap, got a button on top and the scarf to keep the wind out. Proper little man, Mother called me. And she's right. I'm a breadwinner now and proud of it. Got to go. Mustn't be late on my first day.

Lifts his cap and runs off.

BEATY	*(gazing after him)* Dreamy. Looks like Leonardo de Caprio in that ship film, y' know, Titanic.
HUGH	Looks a lot like me I reckon.
BEATY	*(scoffing)* You!

HUGH	Well he is my great grandfather.
BEATY	He's mine too.
CEDD	*(pulls on a jacket and flat cap like **James**'s)* He married your great grandmother young, very young. They had a baby. He went off to fight in the First World War. Never came back. Nearly a million of them never came back. That was the First World War.

Children chant raucously, as in street singing, as they dance.

CHILDREN	When the war is over and the Kaiser's dead
	He's no gaun tae Heaven wi' the eagle on his
	    head
	For the Lord says 'No!' He'll have tae go
	    below
	For he's all dressed up and nowhere tae go.

CEDD	Then a few years later they had a Second World War.

*The **Children** begin doing a conga around the stage, they sing – same tune as before.*

CHILDREN	When the war is over Hitler will be dead
	He hopes to go to Heaven with a crown
	    upon his head
	But the Lord says 'No!' You'll have to go
	    below,
	There's only room for Churchill, so cheery-
	    cheery oh!
	Sounds of siren off and bombs falling.

BEATY	I thought you said things got better for kids.

26

CEDD	They did.
BEATY	There's nothing better about wars, is there? How can wars ever be better?
CEDD:	No, but sometimes wars can make people stop and think a bit – only good thing about them. They know they have to make things better for their grandchildren. Look after them, feed them better. But for some children things didn't always work out as they should, the Jamaican children who came into Britain on the Windrush.
VALERIE	I came on a ship to a place where they said That the milk and honey flowed. The posters had painted a picture of hope, so We decided to travel that road.

The crowds at the docks, when we finally
    landed,
Who cheered and waved from the shore,
In their smiles and their greetings, gave us
    no warning
Of the misery that waited in store.

For the doors which we thought would be
    open in welcome
Were barred and the notices said,
No dogs here, no Irish, WE DO NOT WANT
    BLACKS,
We could not believe what we read.

We were children of Britain, our dads
    fought in the war,
This must be a dreadful mistake
But the cold stares and cold shoulders, the
    insults told us plain,
We'd come to the house of heartache.

At school we were mocked, beaten and spat
on,
The names we were called hard as nails,
But history had taught us that we could be
victors
Though backs were pressed hard on the
rails.

But at least I had one friend, someone who
smiled at me, who took my hand.

*A girl, **Charis**, in pigtails, comes on hopscotching along the
pavement on her way back home from school, (talking to herself).
She sees **Valerie** and takes her hand. They chant (and hand slap,
'pat-a-cake style', the chant faster and faster as they pat).*

VALERIE }
CHARIS }   I hate school dinners. I hate school dinners.
Splishy splashy custard
Dead dogs eyes
All mixed up with giblet pies
Spread it on the butty nice and thick
Swallow it down with a bucket of sick.

*They repeat the verse. From behind the chorus echoes their chant.
Charis and **Valerie** are spooked by the echo. They run off.*

HUGH   Who was that?

CEDD   *(in modern clothes now, baseball cap, Chelsea
shirt etc)* Your grandma and her best friend.
They're still best friends.

HUGH }
BEATY }   Our grandma!

CEDD	Yep. And then after her there was your mum and then you, and after you... That's how it happens, how things keep going. That's why you've got to plant that acorn I gave you. It's what we're here for, to keep things going, make new life, and make things better, if we can.
BEATY	Yes, and we will too.
HUGH	*(kneeling down)* Here? Do I plant it here?
CEDD	Where you like.

Hugh hands the acorn to Beaty and digs with his hands on the edge of the crater. As he does so, the chorus of children from the ages emerge to form a semi-circle about them. Hugh and Beaty do not notice. Beaty kneels now to plant the acorn, and they both fill in the hole, stand up and look down, as if waiting for the tree to grow. Hugh nudges her. The semi-circle has become a circle. He has noticed now they are surrounded by all the children. They feel a little threatened until Cedd, with them in the centre of the circle, reassures them.

CEDD	They've come to say goodbye. We all have. But first they wanted to play a game with you. It's a game they know and you'll know. A game all children have always known. Blindman's Buff.
HUGH	Can I ask you something? Why the shirt? Why Chelsea?
CEDD	They're the champions again, aren't they?
HUGH	How come you know so much?

CEDD	I don't know who's going to win next year, do I?
HUGH	I do. Manchester United.
CEDD	You up for Blindman's Buff? *(Cedd holds out the blindfolds)*
HUGH	Both of us at once?
CEDD	Why not? We can change the rules if we want to, can't we?

He ties the blindfolds on both. Turns them round and round. They begin to grope forwards, arms outstretched, finding each other first. The children in the circle laugh, loving the fun of it. The circle of historical children, hands joined, begin to turn. We hear the distant strains of Boney M. They move to the rhythm of it in a flowing dance, in time synchronised steps. Cedd joins the circle then and after a while leads them off, leaving Hugh and Beaty groping alone on stage. The music is louder now as the children return, in the same costumes now, but as the party children, dancing excitedly, hysterically (hands not joined) as they form the dancing circle again. Cedd is not amongst them. Beaty catches one of them, and then rips off her blindfold. Hugh does the same. They turn around and around wondering. The circle turns into disco dancing. Beaty and Hugh walk through the dancers, to the front of the stage, still wondering about all they've seen. The music dies, the party children dance on in silence now. From amongst them, from the crater, a young tree slowly rises. (A child as a tree) They see it, stop dancing and watch in wonder. Beaty and Hugh turn and see it too. The two join hands, backs to the audience. Children all back away, off stage, reverently, leaving the stage to the tree and Beaty and Hugh. Then, they too leave the stage slowly. The tree stands alone.

Staging and Performing the Play

SET

The author's stage directions at the start of the play provide important information about the design and layout of the stage set:

> *Place: the communal gardens in an appartment block in West London.*
>
> *Centre stage is a great uprooted oak tree, the massive root system facing the audience.*
>
> *Beneath the roots is a large crater.*
>
> *A children's birthday party is in full swing (the children aged between 10 and 12). There's a game of musical chairs going on without the chairs. 25 children are there, in historical costumes of various periods from Anglo-Saxon to medieval to Victorian, except for two, **Hugh** aged 11 dressed as Bart Simpson and his sister **Beaty** dressed as Marge Simpson. Both are wearing easily identifiable cut out cardboard hairpieces.*
>
> (*The Voices of Children*, page 6)

They also indicate some of the challenges which would be faced if a school production attempted to reproduce these requirements exactly as written. Some schools will be able to build scenic elements like the uprooted tree, have a stage with a 'trap' to allow access to the 'crater' from beneath, and provide thirty two historically accurate costumes. However, it would be possible to produce an effective version of this design without these resources by adopting a creative approach to realising the author's stage directions.

The tree is the most important element of the design, because it acts as a visual symbol of a major theme in the play. Cedd, the 'ancestor' of Hugh and Beaty, planted the tree, and, just as the tree has remained standing for over a thousand years, so past generations of children have had the same kinds of experience (of school, hard work, play, suffering etc.) throughout the course of British history. The tree is uprooted at the start of the play, which perhaps suggests that children in Britain today live in a world which has changed to the point where their lives are no longer connected with those of their ancestors. But by listening to the voices of the children of the past – their words as spoken by the characters in the play – we realise that modern children are still linked to children of past ages. A new tree apears at the end of the play to symbolise this continuity.

It might be possible to project an image of an uprooted tree at the beginning of the play, and then replace it with another projection of a young tree at the end. Or you could play around with the idea of the tree, and show an old, dying tree at the start which is replaced by images of trees in blossom or in leaf. The changes could occur at moments when the characters undergo a positive or affirming experience, such as when the children are having fun playing their ring game on pages 19–20, or where Dr. Barnardo offers help to the homeless child on pages 23–24.

Alternatively, you could build a simple tree-like structure: perhaps a pole fixed firmly to the centre of your stage area. Leafy branches could be attached by the characters as they enter, so that by the end of the play what started as a bare trunk has become a flourishing tree in full leaf. This approach would create a similar effect to the author's original intentions, and would be easier to create if your resources are limited.

COSTUME

Some kind of historical costume is essential for most of the characters in this play. Although it will not be necessary to provide all the characters with perfect reproductions of period dress, an attempt should be made to create at least a 'school dressing-up day' appearance for the majority of the children. This is particulary important for the fifteen or so who have speaking parts. Cedd will need the costume in which he first appears, and then six further changes. Some of these will consist of putting a long coat and hat over another set of clothes. However, his costumes will need to be more historically accurate than those of the other children, as Cedd's appearance informs the audience of the historical period in which each section of the play takes place.

EXERCISE
Research and Design

Although no list of costumes is provided, a careful reading of the play will tell you what most of them should look like. Read through the play noting down which character is speaking, and check for any comments from Cedd, stage directions or hints from the text to help you define their historical period. Make a note of whether this is Saxon, Tudor, 18th century etc. Also think about social class. For instance, Alexander and Peter who appear on page 12 are described as being 'well to do'. Their medieval costume will be of higher quality than the Victorian costume of the child factory workers on page 22. There are many books on historical costume available. Use illustrations from these to correspond with your findings, and make some sketches of costume designs based on your research. Think about ways of reproducing these from articles of clothing you may already have around the home.

Most of the speaking roles in *The Voices of Children* are drawn from the group of children who play the party guests in the opening scene. Each character enters to play their short scene, and is then once again absorbed into the group. The danger here is that the play becomes a sort of poetry recital, without any real tension or dramatic interest. In fact, each short scene can be brought to life if the actors have done some background work on their characters. Don't be too concerned about the 'historical' nature of your character. One of the themes of this play is the similarity of feeling and behaviour of children through the ages. Play the character as yourself, but use the exercises below to explore ways of giving added depth to your performance.

EXERCISE

Rehearsing and Acting

- General approach: although the words that you speak may originate in a poem or a piece of text intended to be read rather than performed, think of it as a piece of script to be acted in a believable and realistic manner. Give yourself a *reason* for saying your lines. There are probably several to choose from. For instance, when Geoffrey and Catherine deliver their instructions on good behaviour on pages 13 and 14 they could be:

  a) trying to please their parents, who are listening, in order to get a reward;

  b) being forced to say something that they really don't want to, for fear of punishment;

  c) trying to appear superior to a group of younger children who they are trying to impress.

Try performing the poem with each of these 'intentions'. You should be able to come up with something very different each time. This approach can be used for any speech in the play, and experimenting with different intentions will add variety to your performance.

- Voice: think about the way your character speaks. Is their voice different from your own? What accent does your character have? Do they speak rapidly or slowly? What best suits their personality?

- Movement: how fast or slow does your character move? Is s/he a lazy or active person? Slow-moving or 'bouncy'? Energised or 'laid back'? Go through your part and try out a few different approaches.

- Behaviour: is your character aggressive, confident or passive? Perhaps your first reading of your poem or speech might suggest one or the other, but look for places in the script where an otherwise confident personality could suddenly become timid or scared. An interesting performance is often one where a character behaves in unexpected ways. If the words of your speech or poem suggest that your character is mostly positive and upbeat, try to find places where s/he can show the opposite characteristic. This will make your performance more 'rounded' and true to life.

Girls playing hopscotch in the street, 1897

Children's games are an important feature of *The Voices of Children*. The opening scene of the play features a game of musical chairs, and later, 'drop handkerchief', hopscotch, and blind man's buff are included in the action. A group warm up, featuring some well known playground games, would be useful in setting the right mood for work on this play. Some vigorous game playing before rehearsals will regulate energy levels, and remind you what it feels like to be a young child. Here are a few to choose from:

EXERCISE

- Fox and Rabbit: Choose one person to be Fox and one to be Rabbit. Everyone else finds a partner, stands face to face, and makes a 'rabbit hole' by joining arms, hands holding each other's elbows. Fox and Rabbit start at opposite ends of the playing space. On the signal 'Go', Fox starts to chase Rabbit, who can become 'safe' by standing in any 'hole'. The person to whom Rabbit has his/her back now becomes the new Rabbit. The old Rabbit joins hands with their partner to make a new 'hole'. If Fox catches Rabbit, their roles are reversed.

- Hug Tag: One person is 'it', and tries to tag another member of the group. You can become 'safe' by hugging someone else – but there can only be two people in each hug. You can only get into a hug if in danger of being tagged – otherwise you must keep moving. If the tagger catches someone, they become 'it', and the tagger becomes part of the group being chased.

- Stuck in the Mud: Two people are 'it'. Their objective is to tag every member of the group. This is made possible by the rule that once someone is caught, they stand in one place with their legs apart ('stuck in the mud'). They can be 'released' to rejoin the game when another 'free' player crouches down and passes through their legs. The game continues until everyone is 'stuck'.

Themes in and around the play

SCHOOL DAYS

CEDD   You go to school do you?... Well they
          didn't teach you much, did they?

(The Voices of Children, page 15)

As a boy living in Anglo-Saxon England (about 550–1066 AD) it is
most unlikely that Cedd would have received any formal schooling
as we would understand it today. Until relatively recently, most
children would have spent much of their time helping their parents
and families with various kinds of work. Their 'education' consisted
of learning the skills that would enable them to function in the
work place. Until the late 18th century most people in Britain
worked on the land, and children were an important source of
additional labour on the farm, or in assisting in domestic tasks. In
the late 18th century, when advances in technology led to the
introduction of the manufacturing processes known as the
'Industrial Revolution', many children became wage earners,
working in factories, down coal-mines, or, notoriously as 'climbing
boys' or chimney sweeps.

In medieval times, schooling was provided primarily for the sons of
people who could afford to pay for it. Schools were set up for the
less well off: Winchester College, established in 1382 admitted
seventy 'poor scholars' from the ages of 8 to 12. These scholars
were universally male. Girls from well-off families would be taught
at home. Children were taught to read English and Latin, and if
they continued their education after the age of 12, to write.

Writing was considered to be a specialised skill and not essential to a basic education.

Discipline was always strictly enforced. The poem on page 14 of the play, in which Michael complains of his punishment at the hands of his severe schoolmaster also contains the lines:

> The birchen twigges be so sharpe
> It maketh me have a faint herte.

The 'birchen twigges' or birch twig cane, was used freely as a learning tool until comparatively recently. In 16th century Grammar schools, such as the school in Stratford-upon-Avon that William Shakespeare would have attended as a boy, the Schoolmaster and his teachers (or 'ushers' as they were called) often used physical punishment to keep order and ensure that the boys paid attention to their lessons.

Nobody expected school to be a particularly happy place. With a school day which lasted from six in the morning to five in the afternoon, where Latin and Greek were the only subjects taught, and in which the older boys were permitted to speak *only* in Latin, fear of the cane was the primary method of keeping order. No wonder Shakespeare wrote about:

> …the whining schoolboy, with his satchel
> And shining morning face, creeping like snail
> Unwillingly to school…
>
> (*As You Like It,* Act III Scene I)

Most boys left school at 14. Those from wealthy families might remain for a further two years in preparation for entry into one of the only two universities which existed at that time, Oxford or Cambridge.

A School Day

From the 16th century onwards, education became increasingly available for the less well off. Poorer children whose parents could afford a few pence a week were sent to 'Dame Schools', usually just a room in a cottage, where a local woman would teach the rudiments of reading to children not yet old enough for farm or domestic work.

A segregated Victorian schoolroom

By the 19th century, basic schooling for both boys and girls was becoming more available as charitable organisations set up elementary schools for the poor to teach the 'three Rs': Reading, Writing and Arithmetic. The organisation of classes was very different to anything you might expect today. Children were grouped together in a large room rather than in separate classes, and older children called 'monitors' did much of the teaching. For part of the day, boys and girls were taught separately. Here is an elementary school timetable from 1814:

Morning:

The schools open precisely at nine with prayers ... consisting of the Lord's Prayer and 'the Grace of Our Lord' read by one of the children; and every child not present at prayers, and not assigning a satisfactory reason for absence, is detained after school-hours from five to thirty minutes.

After prayers the first aisle cipher till ten – learn by heart religious exercises till half-past ten – read till eleven – and read till the schools are dismissed at twelve.

Second aisle write till half-past nine – learn religious excercises till ten – read till eleven – and cipher till twelve.

Third aisle learn religious exercises till half past nine – and read and write alternately till twelve.

Afternoon:

The schools re-open at two. The girls school, still in classes with teachers, assistants etc. learn knitting and needle-work till half past four, and arithmetical tables till five.

The boy's school – first aisle cipher till three – write till half past three – read till half past four, – and learn arithmetical tables till five.

Second aisle write till half-past two – read till half past three – cipher till half-past four – and learn arithmetical tables or cipher till five: at which hour both schools are dismissed with the Gloria Patria, sung by the children after prayers read by one of the children.

Thinking and writing

Write out a timetable of your typical schoolday. Compare it with the historical example above. Now think about, and write down ways in which your experience of school differs from that of children in the early 19th century. Consider the following questions:

a) There is an emphasis on religion in the early timetable: those who fail to turn up for prayers are given detention. How does this compare with your school? Why do you think prayers were so important to school authorities at this time?

b) If we understand the word 'cipher' to mean 'maths', how many subjects were these children taught, and what were they?

c) How interesting do you think lessons would have been in those days? Do you think there was any attempt to engage the interest of the children in the subjects taught? Compare this with teaching in your own school.

d) Do you ever have to learn anything 'by heart'? Why do you think this was thought important for children in 1814?

e) The girls are taught knitting and needlework in the afternoon. Why do you think these were thought to be important skills for girls? The boys seem to be doing extra maths and literacy instead. Why would boys need additional time spent in these subjects?

f) The children were taught in 'aisles', an aisle being a long line of desks with a space in between. Each row would have been taught a different subject. Do you think it would be possible to concentrate if several subjects are being taught in the same room at the same time? What about noise levels? Do you think the children were permitted to talk during lessons?

g) Overall, how does your experience of a typical school day compare with that of a child in 1814? Where would you rather be, and why?

Boarding Schools and Board Schools

From *Tom Brown's Schooldays*, published in 1852, to J.K. Rowling's *Harry Potter* series, stories of boarding school life have been extemely popular with children and young adults. Boarding schools for boys whose families could afford them increased in number in in the Victorian period. It was thought that transferring boys of a very young age from their home and family to an all male school environment would produce the kind of 'manly' young men who would be able to govern Britain's expanding empire. Similar establishments were set up for girls, but, then as now, most children experienced boarding school life as fiction.

Books and magazines for children began to appear in larger numbers towards the end of the 19th century. Mandatory education had become the norm for most of the working population of Great Britain, and many children could now read. The government, realising that workers needed to be literate, and fearful of the increase in the numbers of homeless street children in the big cities (one million in 1851) set up 'Board Schools'. School attendance became compulsory. The biggest objection to this change came not from children but from their parents. Until then, children had been available to work to help support the family. Now this source of additional income and domestic assistance was gone. In the 1880s 100,000 parents were prosecuted *each year* for keeping their children out of school!

Discipline was still severe, and beatings were regular occurences. In Manchester in 1911, a group of schoolboys took matters into their own hands and rebelled against this harsh treatment. Larry Goldstone was one of the boys involved. Here is part of his story:

My elder brother was a very popular young man, a real extrovert, and it was him who was the ringleader of the strike at Southall Street school.

You see, the teachers at that time, without any doubt, were sadists. They ruled with fear. They firmly believed in the adage that kids were to be seen and not heard. All they needed was the least excuse and they'd cane you without mercy.

Now when the boys went on strike, they demanded the abolition of the cane, and they also wanted a shilling a week to be paid to the monitors, because they were just used as lackeys. On the big day they met outside the school, over three hundred of them, and they marched to a field opposite the gaol walls of Strangeways. Then they marched along the main road, and threw some stones at the school windows. The strike lasted for three days, but eventually they gave up and returned to school, and all the classes were lined up to witness the punishment of the ringleaders

My brother said they were held over a desk by their outstretched hands and caned on their bottoms. Now, one of the brothers put a plate inside his trousers, and the blow of the cane broke the plate into pieces, badly cutting the lad's bottom. But they come unstuck with my brother. When it came to his turn, he took the teacher by surprise, wrenched the cane from his grasp and started hitting him with it, then he ran out of the school and home.

In the evening, when father came home from work, my brother told him about the canings, and the next morning he went up the school with him. He told the headmaster he didn't approve of the beatings that were carried out at the school, because a lot of the parents were angry when their children told them about the punishments. And he gave the headmaster a strict warning that if anyone dared apply any punishment to his son Jack, then he would go up and mete out far worse to the one responsible. If his lad did anything that required punishment, they were to send a note and he would deal with his son by his own disciplinary methods.

(from *The Penguin Book of Childhood*, ed. Michael Rosen, pp.122–23)

EXERCISE

Drama

In groups, create a series of 4 tableaux (still pictures) which clearly tell the story of the Southall Street demonstration. The school in this acount is a boys school, but if necessary you could imagine it to be co-educational, or transpose the events to a school for girls. Here are some ideas to choose from:

- A school room scene, in which teachers exercise control through fear.

- A meeting of the pupils, in which the ringleader of the strike puts forward his/her ideas.

- The demonstration outside the school.
- The punishment of the ringleaders.
- The brother's revenge.
- The father visits the headmaster.

When devising these frozen images, be aware of the need to show clearly who holds the position of power in each scene, and who is subservient. Think about:

a) Placing on stage: where would you position a character who is supposed to dominate the scene, such as a teacher in the first tableaux, or the father in the last? Experiment with placing dominant characters in different parts of the picture to see which is most effective.

b) Use of physical posture: how would body language reflect the status of those who are in charge, and those who are subservient? How can aggression and fear best be demonstrated using the body alone?

c) Grouping: how would you clearly show the difference between teachers and pupils? Or leaders and followers? Think about how the characters are spaced out in the picture, and how close or distanced they are from each other.

d) Levels: can chairs, tables etc. be used to help you show who holds the power at any particular moment. How do differences in height on stage help to convey differences in status?

To turn these into a short performance pieces, appoint one member as group leader. As the leader counts out aloud from 1 to 6, the performers enter in character and form the first tableaux which will be completed by the final count. This process is then repeated for the other tableaux. Hold each one a little longer than you think necessary before moving on to the next, as the audience need time to fully absorb the image you are presenting.

A teacher beats his pupils

Devised drama/Script writing

Use the tableaux on page 46 to create a devised drama based on the events of the strike. Add dialogue to each of your four scenes to turn the frozen images into a short play. You may want to keep some or all of your ideas on positioning and grouping, if these can be combined effectively with speech. You could devise the dialogue as a group, test it in rehearsal and then write a final script containing the best material.

Remember that the play takes place in 1911. Think about how teachers would have spoken to pupils, fathers to children, and young people to each other, at that time. Try to avoid language or references which are too 'modern'.

Writing

Imagine you are the ringleader of the strike. Write a 'Manifesto' in which you present your ideas for positive change in the running of the school. A manifesto is a 'public declaration of aims' (*Collins English Dictionary*, 2005).

Think clearly about what should be changed. Look at the passage on pages 44–45, and turn the complaints – such as excessive use of the cane – into positive statements, such as 'the use of the cane should be abolished, because...' or 'caning should only be given for...'.

Remember to be clear in the way you express your demands, and to use language which teachers would take seriously rather than too easily dismiss as the moaning of grumpy school kids.

Drama: Hot seating

Take four characters in the Manchester school strike story – Jack Goldstone, the ringleader of the strike, his class teacher, his father and the Headmaster of the school – and 'Hot Seat' them. One person plays the interviewer who is a newspaper reporter from the *Manchester Guardian*. S/He questions each actor in turn, who responds as their character. The reporter asks their opinions of the purpose of schooling: about how well the school is run, their attitudes to discipline, and their role in the strike and its aftermath. The reporter questions them about the success or failure the strike, and what changes, if any, they think need to be made in the school.

Writing

Write a newspaper report in which you recount the story of the strike, and include some of the interview material gained from the Hot Seating exercise above. Decide what 'angle' you are going to take when writing about these events. What kind of readers do you want to please? Those who believe things should stay as they are, and that it is right that schools should maintain a harsh regime? Or will you take a 'crusading' tone, defend the rights of the children and argue that a change in attitude towards discipline is essential?

STREET CHILDREN

Homeless children were not at all uncommon in Victorian England

DR BARNARDO	Do you mean to say my boy that you have no home, that you have no mother or father?
JIM	That's the truth on't Sir. I ain't telling you no lie about it.
DR BARNARDO	But where did you sleep last night?
JIM	Down Whitechapel, Sir, in one of them carts as is filled with 'ay. I won't do 'arm Sir, if you let me stay.
DR BARNARDO	Are there other children sleeping out like you?
JIM	Oh yes lots, 'eaps on 'em, Sir. More'n I could count.

(*The Voices of Children*, page 24)

When in 1870 Dr. Thomas John Barnardo set up his first refuge for homeless children, he was responding to a situation which had been part of British life for hundreds of years. The story of the runaway orphan who escapes from a workhouse and is drawn into a life of crime, is familiar to us from Charles Dicken's *Oliver Twist*. The parish workhouse was supposed to provide food and shelter for destitute people in the 19th century but this was granted in exchange for what was effectively slave-labour. Before the introduction of this system, beggars were often tied to the back of a cart and whipped through the market-place of whichever town they happened to find themselves, before being moved on to the next parish. In 1824 The Vagrancy Act was passed, making it an offence to beg in a public place. The prevailing attitude, which saw poverty and homelessness as crimes which required punishment and control, resulted in children being transported to overseas colonies (North America, Australia) to work as forced labour. The idea was to provide a new environment in which hard work in controlled surroundings would keep them from a 'life of idelnesse'. Shipping children overseas continued in various forms until the 1950s, although in modern times it was seen as a useful method of helping orphaned children find a fresh start in life, rather than as a form of punishment.

Child homelessness became a national problem in the late 1800s, and as we have seen in the section on 'School Days', this concern resulted in the move to compulsory school attendance. Urban populations had expanded massively in the 19th century, as country people moved to the newly industrialised cities in search of factory work. Dreadful living and working conditions – 8-year-old children could work 6 hour factory shifts, and sleep in rooms containing as many as 30 people – meant that some children would rather risk life on the streets as homeless beggars than withstand the severity and overcrowding of a working life. In 1869, the year before the first Barnardo home opened, there were an estimated 100,000 homeless children living rough in the streets of London.

On page 52 there is a first-hand account of the experience of a young girl, collected in London by the journalist Henry Mayhew.

A Victorian flower seller

Mother has been dead just a year this month; she was only bad a fortnight; she suffered great pain, and, poor thing, she used to fret dreadful, as she lay ill, about me, for she knew she was going to leave me. She used to plan how I was to do when she was gone. She made me promise to try to get a place and keep from the streets if I could, for she seemed to dread them so much. When she was gone I was left in the world without a friend. I am quite alone, I have no relation at all, not a soul belonging to me. For three months I went about looking for a place, as long as my money lasted, for mother told me to sell our furniture to keep me and get me clothes. I could have got a place, but nobody would have me without a character, and I knew nobody to give me one. I tried very hard to get one, indeed I did; for I thought of all mother had said to me about going into the streets. At last, when my money was just gone, I met a young woman in the street, and I asked her to tell me where I could get a lodging. She told me to come with her, she would show me a respectable lodging house for women and girls. I went, and I have been there ever since. The women in the house advised me to take to flower-selling, as I could get nothing else to do. One of the young women took me to market with her, and showed me how to bargain with the salesman for my flowers. At first, when I went out to sell, I felt so ashamed I could not ask anybody to buy of me; and many times went back at night with all my stock, without selling one bunch. The woman at the lodging-house is very good to me; and when I have a bad day she will let my lodging go until I can pay her. She always gives me my dinner, and a good dinner it is, of a Sunday; and she will often give me a breakfast, when she knows I have no money to buy any. She is very kind, indeed, for she knows I am alone. I feel very thankful to her, I am sure, for all her goodness to me. ... But I can only sell my flowers five days in the week – Mondays there is no flowers in the market: ...What I shall do in the winter I don't know. In the cold weather last year, when I could get no flowers, I was forced to live on my clothes, I have none left now but what I have on. What I shall do I don't know – I can't bear to think on it.

(Henry Mayhew, *London Labour and the London Poor*
Volume 3, 1851)

Drama

In small groups, use the information in this extract to devise an improvised drama which tells the story of the flower girl. Use the scenes below to help you structure the drama.

Scene 1 – The girl at her mother's death-bed.

Scene 2 – The homeless girl looks for work and is rejected.

Scene 3 – The girl meets the kind flower seller, who helps her to start selling flowers.

Scene 4 – Life in the lodging house.

Scene 5 – The girl at work. She finds it hard to talk to customers, and makes little money.

Scene 6 – The fate of the flower girl: each group discusses the possible fate of the flower girl and decides on an ending to her story.

There are a number of possible outcomes to the story of the flower girl. There were few job opportunities for poor girls in Victorian England. She might manage to find a 'place' as a servant. The work would be arduous and the wages low, but at least she would have a respectable job and a roof over her head.

She might fail as a flower seller, and end up destitute and homeless. She might find work in a factory – but see the section on child labour to find out whether or not this would be a positive outcome. Perhaps, like the heroine of a novel or film, the flower girl might meet a rich benefactor, enabling her to leave street selling and take up a new role in life…

Each group now performs their work. Compare and discuss the alternative endings.

EXERCISE

Writing

- Imagine you are a Victorian campaigner for the rights of homeless children. Re-write the passage above as a letter to your Member of Parliament, demanding that government pass laws to provide for these children. Think about how you could describe the flower girl's problems in a way which emphasised the seriousness of her situation. Perhaps you would downplay the kindness of the lodging house keeper and the other girls, to highlight her predicament.

- In the role of a supporter of the Vagrancy Act of 1824 (see above), use the flower girl's story as the basis of a letter to a newspaper, in which you suggest various methods of dealing with the problem of street children. You might demand:

  a) the building of more workhouses, so that such children can be put to work to pay for their upkeep;

  b) the transportation of homeless children to overseas colonies to work as unpaid labourers;

  or

  c) the building of more prisons so that anyone caught begging could be immediately thrown in jail under the terms of the Vagrancy Act.

Research and writing

In response to problems of child homelessness and poverty, several organisations were set up towards the end of the 19th century to help remedy the situation. As we have seen, one example was the network of children's homes established by Dr. Barnardo. Using books and the internet, (see the 'Further Information' section at the back of this book for details) find answers to the following questions about the work of the Barnardo homes:

- Who was Dr. Barnardo? Describe the social conditions in London that led him to begin his work with homeless children.

- What event led to the sign 'No destitute child ever refused admission' being placed outside every Home?

- What kind of help did the first Barnardo Homes provide?

- How did the work of the Barnardo Homes change after the Second World War? What changes occurred in society to make orphanages less necessary?

- How does the help provided by Barnardos in the 21st century differ from the type of assistance offered when the homes were originally set up?

- Now use your findings to write a short report on the history of this organisation.

CHILDREN AT WORK

CEDD Do you know the saddest story I ever heard? It was about a factory girl who had to get up early every morning to go to work. One morning she was sick, too weak to get up. She was lying in her father's arms. She woke up and the first thing she thought was that it must be time to go to work. "Father is it time?" she said. "Father, is it time?" Then she sank back in his arms and died.

(*The Voices of Children*)

Throughout much of the period covered by *The Voices of Children*, most young people were expected to work to help support their parents and families. For the 70% of the population of Great Britain who did not belong to the upper or middle classes, the notion that childhood after the age of 7 was a time for carefree fun and play would have seemed strange, at least to generations living before the late 1800s. It was during the middle of the 19th century that exploitation of children in the workplace became most severe. The noise, dirt, drudgery and exhaustion to which children were subjected as factory and mine workers at this time led reformers to lobby for changes in the law to protect child labourers. Joseph Hebergam, a seven year old working in a Huddersfield spinning mill worked from 5 am to 8 pm with a daily break of 30 minutes. An overseer, armed with a leather strap patrolled the factory, hitting any child who failed to work at the required speed. Joseph later reported 'I wished many times they could have sent me for a West India slave ... I thought ... that there could not be worse slaves than those who worked in factories'. Many children were injured by the machinery. A young mill worker called Robert Blincoe had his finger severed by a spinning frame wheel:

he clapped the mangled joint, streaming with blood, to the finger, and ran off to... the surgeon, who, very composedly, put the parts together again, and sent him back to the mill. Though the pain was so intense he could scarcely help crying out every minute, he was not allowed to leave the frame.

A girl spinning wool at Foster's Mill, Bradford, in 1902

'Father, is it time?'

The slogan 'Father, is it time?' was carried by protestors whose complaints against the cruel treatment of children in the workplace resulted in the passing of the Factory Act of 1833. This restricted working hours for children under 13 to 9 hours per day, and for 13–18-year-olds to 11 hours per day. The fact that many *adult* workers in modern Britain work around 8 hours per day emphasises the hardship that these young people were forced to undergo. Children working underground in coal mines experienced similar misery. Working naked, with very little light, children as young as 7 were employed to open and close the air vents in the mineshafts. Those a little older were harnessed to carts, to transport the coal from the coalface to the surface. Under the increasing pressure of public opinion, a number of further laws were passed to limit the exploitation of child labour. The Factory Act of 1878 finally prevented the employment of any child under 10 years of age, and provided schooling for children of employees.

Boys working in the coal mine

The Climbing Boys

The speech given to the climbing boy George on page 21 of *The Voices of Children* conveys some of the unpleasant aspects of the short life of an apprentice chimney sweep. Many such boys were sold by their parents at a young age, to masters who made them sleep in cellars on the bags of soot from the chimneys they had swept. They were sometimes forced to crawl up chimneys only nine inches square, made to work naked to avoid the need to spend money on new clothes, and were rarely allowed to bathe. This often caused fatal skin cancer. Burns and respiratory illness were other common causes of their often premature deaths, which usually occurred within a few years of starting work. Such children were social outcasts. They were sometimes even refused admittance to church services. The poet William Blake, who experienced the harshness of child labour at first hand, having been employed as a boy to work 12 hour shifts in a silk mill, wrote two contrasting poems, both entitled 'The Chimney Sweeper'. The first poem is included in a collection of poems called *Songs of Innocence*, published in 1794. In the third line of the poem the boy cries ' 'weep! 'weep!'. This represents both the traditional street cry of the climbing boy – 'sweep, sweep' – as heard in the distance, and also the word 'weep', to cry.

THE CHIMNEY SWEEPER

When my mother died I was very young,
And my father sold me while yet my tongue
Could scarcely cry 'weep! 'weep! 'weep! 'weep!
So your chimneys I sweep, and in soot I sleep.

There's little Tom Dacre, who cried when his head,
That curled like a lamb's back, was shaved: so I said,
'Hush, Tom! never mind it, for when your head's bare,
You know that the soot cannot spoil your white hair.'

And so he was quiet; and that very night,
As Tom was a-sleeping, he had such a sight, –
That thousands of sweepers, Dick, Joe, Ned, and Jack,
Were all of them locked up in coffins of black.

And by came an angel who had a bright key,
And he opened the coffins and set them all free;
Then down a green plain leaping, laughing, they run,
And wash in a river, and shine in the sun.

Then naked and white, all their bags left behind,
They rise upon clouds and sport in the wind;
And the angel told Tom, if he'd be a good boy,
He'd have God for his father, and never want joy.

And so Tom awoke; and we rose in the dark,
And got with our bags and our brushes to work.
Though the morning was cold, Tom was happy and warm;
So if all do their duty they need not fear harm.

William Blake

A Victorian chimney sweep

Reading and Understanding

- Read through the poem several times and write down or discuss your first thoughts about it.

- Do you think the message of the poem is essentially positive? What is the meaning of the last line 'if all do their duty they need not feel harm'?

- One explanation of this line is that 'hard work brings its own reward'. Do you think this is true for the climbing boys?

- Do you think that it is a sentimental poem written for the purpose of getting children to do what they are told?

- Is it about someone who is trying to find some good even in the worst circumstances?

- Is it a sad poem in which the unhappy life of the chimney sweep is brightened for a short time by a dream of happiness?

- Could the phrase 'coffins of black' in the third verse mean more than just the coffins in which the dead are buried? Think about the conditions in which the sweeps worked: the amount of light they have, the substance they are working with, and their appearance when they come back down the chimney.

- How many times are words associated with 'blackness', 'whiteness' or 'brightness' mentioned in the poem?

- What good and bad qualities or feelings are associated with 'blackness' and 'brightness' in the poem?

- Is Tom Dacre's dream about death? Is his dream a vision of heaven? If so, what does this tell us about the chances of a sweep finding happiness while they are alive?

- Look again at the information on page 59 about the dreadful conditions in which the climbing boys worked. Remember that the author and the original readers of the poem would have been very familiar with these facts, and would encounter climbing boys in the streets of their towns and cities. Re-read the poem, keeping this in mind.

- Do you think the poem could be ironic? When we read the poem, we are aware that the narrator of the poem and his fellow sweeps will shortly fall victim to illness and death. Does this put us in a position where we know more than the child who narrates the poem?

- If this is so, do you think that the boy's simple faith in future happiness, as expressed in the dream, is an illusion? Will the sweeps ever really be set free from their 'coffins of black'?

- Do you think the poet intends us to think there is any kind of 'happy ending' to this poem?

- Why do you think the poem was included in a book called *Songs of Innocence*?

Children at work in modern Britain

It would a mistake to think that child labour ended at the end of the 19th century. Research undertaken in the 1990s showed that:

…between one third and one half of children aged 13 to 15 were in some form of paid employment. Some of them worked in jobs that had long been designated as being for children, like delivering newspapers, but others worked in shops, hotels, door-to-door selling, garages and building sites. A significant minority of these children, perhaps as many as a quarter, worked more than 10 hours a week, on top of 30 hours at school.

(Hugh Cunningham, *The Invention of Childhood*, pp.221–22)

EXERCISE

Discussion

- Do you or any of your friends do any kind of paid work? If so, what kind of work is it?

- Why do you work? Is it just to earn pocket money?

- What do you use the money for? Do your wages supplement other pocket money?

- How many hours a week do you think children should work?

- Do you think that working to earn extra money could have a bad effect on your school work?

- Do you do any other form of unpaid work, other than school work?

- Do you think it is a good thing for young adults to have some experience of paid work before they leave full-time education? If so, why?

VOICES FROM OTHER LANDS

For much of the time-period covered by *The Voices of Children*, Britain had become a home for children of other lands. Cedd, the Anglo-Saxon boy, is a representative 'ancestor' figure to the future generations of children whose voices are heard in the play. However, Cedd's people were also immigrants. The Anglo-Saxons were a mixture of peoples from the coastal regions of northern

Europe, who, through a combination of armed conquest and peaceful integration, settled in Britain in the fifth century AD. From medieval times onwards, Britain has become a destination for people of many different races, cultures and nations, searching for new opportunities and freedom from oppression. Britain's current multi-cultural society has been in the making for hundreds of years.

Prominent among immigrant groups arriving in London in the 19th century were the Irish, fleeing from the devastation caused by the great famine of 1845. In that year, the potato crop, the staple diet of many Irish workers, failed. Mass starvation and illness resulted in an estimated one million deaths, and many of the survivors fled overseas, some settling in Britain. Towards the end of the century, Jewish refugees from Russia arrived. They were fleeing from the 'Pogroms' – the government sanctioned destruction of Jewish homes. These attacks, and the murderous riots which followed, led to the deaths of thousands of innocent men, women and children.

Black Britons

Records of people of African descent living in Britain go back nearly 2000 years, (before the period covered in this play) when African soldiers in the Roman army were stationed in what was then the Roman province of Britannia. Small numbers of black people lived and worked in Britain in the 17th and 18th centuries, and by the middle of the 19th century, black communities were established in the seaports of London, Bristol, Liverpool and Cardiff.

However, the black population expanded considerably after World War II, when the government invited people from former British colonies in Africa and the Caribbean to move to Britain to work. In many cases, parents emigrated first, and then sent for their children once they had established a home in the UK. Life was not easy for many of these families. They suffered from racial discrimination by employers and landlords. Black workers could be paid less than their white counterparts, and a common sign outside rented accommodation in the 1950s was 'No Blacks or Irish'.

The well known TV comedian, Lenny Henry, remembers his early years as the child of Afro-Caribbean parents growing up in Dudley in the West Midlands:

I can remember this place called Victoria Terrace, which was a big old house that was our first proper home …We had an outside toilet …you'd walk to the toilet freezing cold. I remember falling over in the snow once, when I was about four or five and cutting my hand on broken glass in the backyard. I remember the kid next door, William, who was my best friend – you always had a best friend – but he always had loads and loads of toys. This white guy befriended me, but would just turn off the friendship and, you know, I'd go and call for him and I'd shout, then he'd spit through the letterbox at me. Things like that, you know. And it would be on a whim. You know, one day I'd be his best friend, the next day I'd be that blackie who lives next door. So I had one of those strange relationships, but generally in that house, we had very, very good times.

(from M. Philips and T. Phillips, *Windrush: The Irresistible Rise of Multi-racial Britain*, p.208)

Discussion

- How do you explain the actions of the white boy in the passage above? Why do you think someone would veer between friendliness and abuse in this way?

- Various groups within society are subject to the prejudiced or intolerant opinions of others. These could include attitudes which are racist, sexist or disparaging towards particular social groups, particularly those who are seen as being in some way 'different' from the majority. Why do you think people who are in minority groups of one kind or another, or who choose to behave in a way which is different from the majority, are sometimes subjected to treatment which is intolerant or abusive?

- Do you think that expressing such beliefs could create a situation of conflict within a society as a whole?

- Should people be allowed to express prejudiced attitudes, regardless of the consequences? Is freedom of speech more important than the hurt such remarks could cause?

British Asians

Many different cultural and ethnic groups live in 21st century Britain. One of the largest is the South Asian group, consisting of people from India, Pakistan or Bangladesh. The earliest arrivals were the Roma (or Gypsies, as they are often known) who left Northern India and Pakistan around 1000 AD, and had settled in Britain by the 17th century.

Small communities of South Asians, the descendants of sailors and domestic servants were increased in the 1950s and '60s when manual workers from Northern India, Pakistan and Bangladesh were encouraged to move to Britain to fill the shortage of labour following World War II. At the same time, many qualified medical staff arrived from India, to take up jobs in the newly created National Health Service.

In the late 1960s and early 70s, South Asians who held British passports and who had already emigrated to African countries such as Uganda and Kenya, settled in Britain, having been forcibly expelled by the governments of those countries.

British Asians have experienced many of the same problems as their Black British counterparts. In fact most immigrant groups in Britain, both white and non-white, have experienced discrimination of one kind or another. The Race Relations Act of 1976 made it illegal to discriminate against anyone on grounds of colour, nationality, race or ethnic origin.

Childhood Memories

Here is a poem written by a 12-year-old boy, Tanweer Khaled, whose family had settled in London. The poem is a vivid description of his family home in Bangladesh.

My Memories

Bangladesh
I remember going to my village home
I remember it being hot
I remember the sole of my shoes
burning up on the hot road
I remember jumping about because
of my hot foot
I remember my little brother
running up to my grandparents
on his little feet like an ant
I remember my little brother
jumping on my grandfather's lap
and my grandfather nearly falling
off the chair
I remember having a nice meal
I remember my brother eating
the leg of a chicken like a lion
eating a deer
I remember the homemade oven
I remember...I remember
I remember...I remember BANGLADESH

(from *The Penguin Book of Childhood*,
ed. Michael Rosen, pp.181–82)

Researching and writing.

○ Read the poem several times. How many different 'images' or 'scenes' appear in the poem? Make a list of these.

○ What senses are evoked in the poem (e.g. taste, smell etc.)? Make a note of each.

○ In pairs, take turns to tell each other a story about an early memory, something that was important to you. This could be a significant life event or just something ordinary. Give as much detail as you can about the events which occurred.

○ Describe your *emotional* reactions to the memory: contentment, anxiety, excitement etc.

○ Also describe the *sense experiences* connected with the memory. Think about visual images, sounds, tastes and smell.

○ Now:

   a) Write an account of either your experience or that of your partner, giving as much factual detail as possible

   b) Write an account of either your experience or that of your partner, giving as much sensory and emotional detail as possible.

○ Which of the two is the most interesting? Why is this?

○ A good piece of creative writing often describes not just the events which occurred, or the emotions that they evoked, but also how the writer or characters responded to the situation in terms of visual images, sounds, tastes and smells. Go back to your two versions and combine them to tell the story of your significant memory, blending information, emotion and sensory experiences.

Further information

An excellent general guide to the history of children in Britain is *The Invention of Childhood*, by Hugh Cunningham, published by BBC Books.

SCHOOL DAYS

There are several books which feature descriptions of boarding schools in the Victorian period. *Nicholas Nickleby* by Charles Dickens features the ghastly Dotheboys Hall, ruled over by the tyrannical headmaster Wackford Squeers. *Tom Brown's School Days* by Thomas Hughes is a portrait of life at Rugby School, in which the hero, Tom Brown, encounters the vicious school bully, Flashman. Although works of fiction, both are based to some extent on the realities of school life in mid-19th century Britain.

For a view of a different type of schooling, *Cider With Rosie* by Laurie Lee describes the author's childhood in a Gloucestershire village just after the First World War.

STREET CHILDREN

Oliver Twist by Charles Dickens is the classic tale of a runaway orphan who falls into a life of crime. There have been several film versions. The best was made in 1948, and was directed by David Lean. Many people are familiar with the musical version, *Oliver!*, which became a highly successful film.

Information about Dr. Barnardo and his work can be found at: www.barnardos.org.uk

The full text of *London Labour and the London Poor* by the Victorian journalist, Henry Mayhew, which contains a huge amount of information and interview material about life on the streets in 19th century London, can be found at the *Tufts Digital Library* website.

For a contemporary view of homelessness, *Homebird*, a play by Terence Blacker is a humorous story of Nicky, a teenager on the run.

CHILDREN AT WORK

The BBC History website has a useful section on children at work, play and in school: www.bbc.co.uk/history/forkids

VOICES FROM OTHER LANDS

A useful website, providing information about the experiences of children emigrating to Britain is: www.movinghere.org.uk

WHO DO YOU THINK YOU ARE?

You might like to start tracing the story of your own family. A good place to start would be the BBC History Family History site on www.bbc.co.uk/history/familyhistory